# The Wheel of
# DECEPTION

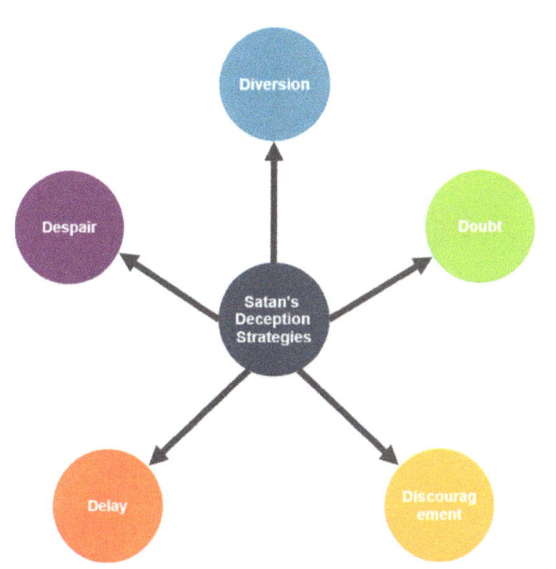

## Madison C. Brown

Copyright © 2024 Madison C. Brown
All rights reserved
First Edition

NEWMAN SPRINGS PUBLISHING
320 Broad Street
Red Bank, NJ 07701

First originally published by Newman Springs Publishing 2024

ISBN 979-8-89308-808-3 (Paperback)
ISBN 979-8-89308-809-0 (Digital)

Printed in the United States of America

# CONTENTS

Preface ..................................................................................v
Chapter 1: I Am a Citizen of the Kingdom of God ......................1
Chapter 2: Deception Characterizes the Enemy ..........................8
Chapter 3: The Wheel of Deception .........................................13
Chapter 4: Wheel of Deception: Out of Service ........................28

# PREFACE

This work is a revelation I received from the Lord over a decade ago. It has taken me years to distill this insight into writing. During this incubation period, I have sought to teach the concept of the "Wheel of Deception" to local churches, emphasizing how our enemy values organization and uses strategic deception against us.

It's alarming how our society increasingly values deception. Take, for instance, the old game show *To Tell the Truth*, where the objective was to identify the one truthful contestant among two liars. Today, it feels like our society has begun to favor liars. We encounter terms like "alternative truths," especially in the political arena, causing division and conflict.

The Bible is clear about God's stance on deception. Proverbs 6:16–19 lists the things God hates, including a lying tongue and a false witness who speaks lies. As believers, we must be vigilant against these deceitful tactics that aim to disrupt and destroy our lives.

The key learning I received from the revelation was that the enemy uses the "Wheel of Deception" to systematically cause chaos in our lives. If you find yourself entangled in this wheel, I pray that the Spirit of the Lord will guide you, as He did me, to recognize and combat these strategies of the enemy.

Finally, allow me to be intrusive for a moment. If you have not yet accepted God's salvation by believing in His Son, Jesus, I pray that the Spirit of the Lord will speak to you through this work. Jesus says, "I stand at the door and knock. If anyone hears my voice and opens the door, I will come in" (Revelation 3:20). As you read this writing, I hope you hear Jesus knocking and feel inspired to open the door to Him.

—Pastor Brown

CHAPTER 1

# I Am a Citizen of the Kingdom of God

Being citizens of the kingdom of God resonates deeply with the essence of Christian faith and understanding. This powerful revelation requires an open heart and mind to fully grasp it. Allowing the Word of God to enlighten our understanding is crucial to embracing our identity as citizens of God's kingdom. Sometimes, it means unlearning certain preconceived notions or misconceptions and being open to the leading of the Holy Spirit.

Learning to listen with our spirit is key to receiving the deeper truths and revelations contained in God's Word. Through this spiritual discernment, we can fully comprehend the original precepts and thoughts of the Word, leading to insightful enlightenment and transformation.

Experiencing a consistent move of the Spirit of God in our lives is evidence of our citizenship in His kingdom. Through the indwelling presence of the Holy Spirit, we are guided, empowered, and protected from the traps of deception that seek to ensnare us. Our journey toward this understanding testifies to the transformative power of God's Word and Spirit.

This ongoing process of growth and revelation continually deepens our relationship with God and our understanding of His kingdom. Have you noticed how each new insight, each moment of clarity, brings you closer to His truth? A friend's unexpected help during a difficult time felt like a beam of divine light, piercing through confusion and doubt. Each such instance, no matter how small, should draw us nearer to God's eternal wisdom and love.

This transformation is a powerful reminder of the Spirit's work within us, shaping us into true citizens of God's kingdom. Every revelation, every moment of understanding, is like a sculptor's chisel, refining our souls and aligning us with His purpose.

Understanding ourselves as citizens of the kingdom of God transforms how we perceive ourselves and our relationship with Him. This transformation is more than just a shift in perspective; it is a deep, ongoing process that shapes our identity and strengthens our bond with the Divine. I can testify, that I remember moments of doubt and uncertainty, and while in the midst of this faith dilemma, the Spirit of the Lord reveals how God uses these moments to bring us closer to a fuller understanding of His love and guidance. There were times when the path seemed shrouded in uncertainty, and my faith wavered. But then, like a beacon in the fog, moments of clarity emerged. I remember sitting quietly one evening, overwhelmed with confusion, when suddenly a sense of peace washed over me—a gentle assurance of His presence and direction.

A valuable habit in our lives is to occasionally reflect on those instances of divine intervention in our lives. It may have been a kind word from a stranger when you needed it most, a prayer answered in an unexpected way, or a scripture passage that spoke directly to your heart. Each of these experiences is a testament to the Spirit's work within us, guiding us closer to God's truth and love. These reflections not only deepen our understanding but also strengthen our faith, reminding us that we are continually being shaped into true citizens of God's kingdom. Embrace these moments, and let them affirm the transformative power of His grace in your life. Every insight is a testament to God's enduring presence and the Spirit's work within us. Would you agree with me when I say the only thing we can say is "Glory to His name for this incredible, life-changing journey!"

As we see ourselves maturing in the grace of our God, we must not become naïve to the enemy's desire to ship-wreck our journey. The "Wheel of Deception" is an apt metaphor for the cycles of con-

# THE WHEEL OF DECEPTION

fusion and misunderstanding that can ensnare us if we're not vigilant. This powerful image illustrates how the enemy seeks to keep us trapped in patterns of thought that hinder our spiritual growth and prevent us from fully embracing the truth of God's kingdom. As Paul highlights in 2 Corinthians 4:3–4, the spiritual battle we face involves the enemy blinding us to the truth of the gospel.

However, through seeking enlightenment and revelation from God, we can break free from this deception and walk in the light of His truth. Our journey serves as a reminder of the importance of continually seeking deeper understanding and allowing the Holy Spirit to illuminate our hearts and minds. By doing so, we break the cycle of deception and move closer to the fullness of God's kingdom. Paul's words to the Philippians encapsulate the transformative nature of our salvation and citizenship in the kingdom of God. When we accept Christ as our Savior, we experience an extraordinary spiritual renewal that changes our identity and our destiny. Being citizens of high heaven means that our ultimate allegiance and identity are rooted in the heavenly realm. While we currently reside on earth, our true citizenship is in heaven, and we eagerly anticipate the return of our Savior, Jesus Christ, who will complete the work of transformation that He has begun in us. The promise of our earthly bodies being transformed into glorious bodies like Christ's own speaks to the ultimate fulfillment of our salvation. Not only will our souls be redeemed, but our physical bodies will also be renewed and glorified, reflecting the perfection and beauty of our Savior. This transformation is not just a future hope but a present reality that begins the moment we accept Christ. Through the indwelling presence of the Holy Spirit, we are continually being transformed into the image of Christ, becoming more like Him in character and conduct. This ongoing transformation reminds us that our hope is both present and future, rooted in the unshakable promise of God's kingdom. Through every step, the Holy Spirit shapes us, preparing us for the ultimate glorification that awaits us in Christ. Our citizenship in heaven stems from the redemptive work of Jesus Christ on the cross. Through His sacrifice, He reconciled us to God and made it possible for us to become citizens of His kingdom. When we confess Jesus as our Lord and Savior, believing in our hearts that God raised Him from the dead, we are born again into this heavenly citizenship. This act of faith is our naturalization process, wherein we are adopted into the family of God and become heirs to His promises. It's a demonstration of God's grace and mercy that He would offer us such a privilege, despite who we might have been. Yes, God desires for us to be part of His heavenly kingdom and to share in the benefits and blessings that come with citizenship. I remember the moment I truly grasped this incredible gift and how it transformed my understanding and my life. It's a humbling reminder of God's boundless love and the incredible honor of being part of His kingdom. Through His sacrifice, we not only receive forgiveness but are also invited to share in the fullness of His grace. This is the essence of our faith: a continual journey of understanding and embracing the depth of God's grace and our place in His heavenly family.

Our confession of faith in Jesus Christ marks the beginning, transforming us from citizens of this world to citizens of heaven and granting us access to the abundant life promised. Ultimately, our citizenship in heaven is a testament to God's unfailing love and His desire for a restored relationship with us. It's a privilege that carries with it the responsibility to live according to the values and principles of God's kingdom, bringing His light and love to the world around us. Giving thanks to God for making us citizens of heaven is not only appropriate but essential. Understanding the depth of what God has done for us and how He accomplished it is crucial. The passage from the Colossians expresses the reality of our salvation. God, in His infinite grace and mercy, rescued us from the kingdom of darkness, where we were separated from Him. Through the sacrificial death of Jesus Christ, God transferred us into the kingdom of His dear Son, where we now have forgiveness of sins and the promise of eternal life. This act of redemption is solely the work of God. He initiated the process of our naturalization into His kingdom, making it possible for us to share in the inheritance of His people who live in the light. It's a testament to His love and His desire for us to be reconciled to Him and to experience the fullness of life found in our relationship with Him.

Reflecting on our past lives in the kingdom of darkness, where we were guided by our own desires and limited understanding, serves as a powerful reminder of the magnitude of God's grace in rescuing us. I remember days when my heart was heavy, burdened by the weight of my own choices. The darkness felt like an unending night, with no dawn in sight. But then, a whisper of grace broke through. Slowly, the shadows receded, replaced by a light so powerful that it changed everything. Think of those moments, both big and small, where you felt His presence. Reflect and remember your journey from darkness to light. It's through His intervention that we are now eligible to receive the blessings and promises of His kingdom. Giving thanks to God for His work in our lives is not just a response to His goodness but also a recognition of His sovereignty and His power to transform us from sinners to saints. It's an act of worship and gratitude for His unmerited favor and love toward us.

Paul taught the Colossians that God made us "meet" to be partakers of the inheritance of the saints. The word "meet" in this passage carries with it the concept of being "enabled" or "qualified." In other words, through the finished work of the Lord Jesus Christ and our belief and acceptance of Him as our Savior, God made us qualified. The meaning of "qualified" in Colossians 1:12 reveals to us the depth of God's grace and the significance of what He has done for us through Jesus Christ. It's an undisputable truth that we, in and of ourselves, could never do enough to qualify for the inheritance of the saints. It's only through the redemptive work of Jesus Christ—His sacrifice on the cross—that we are made worthy and qualified to partake in the blessings of God's kingdom. Our qualification has blood on it—the precious blood of Jesus Christ—underscoring the price that was paid for our redemption. It's through His shed blood that our sins are forgiven and our relationship with God is restored. Accepting Jesus as our Lord and Savior is what enables God to qualify us as citizens of His kingdom. Now that we are citizens of His kingdom, it's critical that we abandon thoughts of unworthiness. Dwelling on such thoughts undermines the reality of God's grace and diminishes the significance of Christ's sacrifice. God has made us new creatures in Christ, and through Him, we have access to the fullness of God's kingdom and all its blessings. Let's continually remind ourselves of the transformative power of Christ's sacrifice and live fully in the reality of our heavenly citizenship. The kingdom of God is our inheritance, restored to us through Jesus Christ. When God invaded the enemy's territory to rescue us, it was a decisive and powerful act of redemption. Perhaps you have experienced the feeling of violation when someone trespasses on your personal space; the enemy experienced a similar intrusion when God intervened to save us. God disarmed the enemy and nullified his power over us. It's true; the enemy is indeed angry and determined to wreak havoc in our lives. The enemy's goal is to destroy us, whether through external influences, such as other people or substances, or through our own self-destructive behaviors. The enemy's tactics may vary, but his objective remains the same—to steal, kill, and destroy. Jesus' warning to Peter about the devil's desire to sift him as wheat serves as a sobering reminder of the spiritual battle we face. We must remain vigilant and aware of the enemy's schemes, relying on God's strength and protection to resist his attacks. I am cognizant that it seems as though the enemy is relentless, but let's settle with the fact that God is greater. Let's continually seek God's strength and remain vigilant, knowing that our inheritance in His kingdom is secure and His protection is unwavering.

*The Wheel of Deception* is just one of the many tools the enemy uses to deceive and ensnare us. Recognizing this reality is the first step in guarding ourselves against his tactics and standing firm in our faith. The "Wheel of Deception," with its five cycles representing diversion, doubt, discouragement, delay, and despair, provides a framework for understanding the strategies the enemy employs to lead us away from God's truth and purposes.

*Diversion.* The enemy seeks to distract us with seemingly urgent but ultimately unimportant matters, pulling our focus away from God's plans. For example, constant busyness can divert our attention from prayer and Bible study.

*Doubt.* He plants seeds of doubt in our minds, causing us to question God's goodness and promises. Remember how Eve was tempted in the Garden of Eden with the question, "Did God really say…?"

*Discouragement.* The enemy uses setbacks and failures to dishearten us, making us feel inadequate and unworthy of God's love. Consider times when a single failure made you question your entire worth.

*Delay.* He introduces delays in our lives, making us feel like God's promises will never come to pass. This can lead to impatience and frustration, causing us to act outside of God's timing.

*Despair.* Ultimately, the enemy aims to bring us to a place of despair where we feel hopeless and disconnected from God's grace. It's crucial to remember that God's light is always present, even in our darkest moments.

I can remember seasons in my life when the enemy offered these tactics to lead me astray. There were times when doubt whispered lies into my heart, when fear clouded my judgment, and when temptation tried to pull me away from my faith. Yet, God caused me to recognize these strategies for what they were—attempts to divert me from God's path. Identifying and understanding these tactics is crucial to standing firm. By remaining vigilant and grounding ourselves in God's Word, we can resist the "Wheel of Deception."

As kingdom citizens, let's commit to staying focused on God's truth, trusting in His timing, and leaning on His strength to overcome discouragement and despair. Now that we are aware of the enemy's schemes, we can actively guard against them and remain steadfast in our faith.

CHAPTER 2

# Deception Characterizes the Enemy

> Ye are of your father the devil, and the lusts of your father ye will do.
> —John 8:44

He was a murderer from the beginning, and abode not in the truth, because there is no truth in him. "When he speaketh a lie, he speaketh of his own: for he is a liar, and the father of it." This verse is part of a dialogue between Jesus and a group of Jews who were questioning His identity and teachings. In this passage, Jesus makes a strong statement about their actions and spiritual alignment. Let's break down the verse for a clearer understanding: "Ye are of your father the devil, and the lusts of your father ye will do." Jesus is accusing these individuals of following the devil's desires and inclinations. He implies that their actions and motivations are aligned with evil rather than with God. This accusation is a stark contrast to their claim of being Abraham's descendants and spiritually aligned with God. Jesus is saying that their actions reflect those of the devil, whom He identifies as their spiritual father. "He was a murderer from the beginning, and abode not in the truth, because there is no truth in him." This likely alludes to the story of Cain and Abel in Genesis 4, where Cain's murder of Abel is seen as inspired by evil. It also references the devil's role in bringing death into the world through the deception of Adam and Eve, leading to their spiritual death (Genesis 3).

The devil's nature is described as fundamentally deceitful. Unlike God, who embodies truth, the devil is inherently false and deceptive. His rebellion against God is characterized by a rejection of truth. "When he speaketh a lie, he speaketh of his own: for he is a liar, and the father of it." Lying is inherent to the devil's nature. When he lies, he is acting according to his character. This statement underscores the devil's role as the originator and perpetuator of lies. By calling the devil "the father of it," Jesus emphasizes that all lies originate from him. This description highlights the contrast between the devil and God, who is the source of all truth. Jesus uses strong language to emphasize the moral and spiritual corruption of those he addresses, contrasting their behavior with the truth and righteousness that come from God. This verse highlights the seriousness of aligning oneself with falsehood and evil, underscoring the spiritual battle between truth and deception. Jesus condemns hypocrisy and deceit, urging these people to embrace honesty and integrity. This powerful message serves as a reminder of the constant struggle between good and evil in our own lives, challenging us to reflect on our actions and strive for righteousness. 1 Peter 5:8 instructs us to have a "sound mind" in understanding the enemy and his tactics. Jesus is emphatic and literal when He states that the enemy, the thief, seeks total destruction. The Spirit of the Lord directed Paul to write: "Be sober, be vigilant; because your adversary the devil, as a roaring lion, walketh about, seeking whom he may devour." Here, "sober" means to be of sound mind, "vigilant" means to be watchful, and "adversary" refers to our opponent. The Word of God is clear: the enemy is the devil, and he is our opponent, whose goal is our destruction by 'any means necessary'. This verse underscores the importance of mental clarity and constant vigilance in our spiritual lives. By maintaining a sound mind and being watchful, we can recognize and resist the devil's attempts to lead us astray.

In today's world, this means staying alert to negative influences and deceptive practices that seek to undermine our faith and integrity. "Any means necessary" can be understood to encompass a wide range of tactics and strategies the devil may employ to achieve his goal of destruction. You may agree with me and testify that we have seen some of these things.

Doctrinal and scriptural manipulation is designed to lead us away from the truth of the gospel (2 Corinthians 11:13–15), causing confusion and doubt (2 Peter 3:16). Moral and ethical corruption with the intent to lure us into sinful behaviors (James 1:14–15); temptation to shift our focus from spiritual priorities to wealth, power, or other material gains (1 Timothy 6:9–10). Disruption of unity, sowing discord, weakening the unity and effectiveness of the church (Proverbs 6:16–19), causing misunderstandings, and fostering jealousy among the men and women of God (James 3:16). Psychological and emotional attacks are engineered to dissuade us from following Christ through suffering (1 Peter 4:12–13). Using fear, anxiety, and depression causes destabilization (2 Timothy 1:7). Spiritual doubts and despair challenge us to question God's existence (Genesis 3:1–5). Distractions keep us busy with matters that seem somewhat important; distracting us with worldly concerns prevents growth (Luke 10:41–42).

Thanks to God, our Father, for the victory in Jesus Christ, our Lord. We have the fullness of the Godhead at our disposal to counter every tactic. In 2 Corinthians 2:11, Paul warns us to stay vigilant against Satan's devious plans, reminding us that awareness and preparedness are our shields against his attempts to gain an upper hand. "Lest Satan should get an advantage of us: for we are not ignorant of his devices." By stating, "we are not ignorant of his devices," Paul emphasizes that believers should be vigilant and aware of Satan's strategies and tactics." "The New Testament repeatedly portrays Satan as a destroyer, whose purpose is to steal, kill, and destroy. This theme is powerfully outlined by Jesus: "The thief cometh not, but for to steal, and to kill, and to destroy; I am come that they might have life, and that they might have it more abundantly." Recognizing and understanding the enemy's methods, whether it's deception, temptation, division, or persecution, he will not operate from an advantageous position. You and I are kingdom citizens, and we have God's prevailing power to be more than conquerors. Yes, the enemy has a strategy, but so do we. Here's ours:

1. Stay spiritually alert and watchful, knowing that the enemy can use both subtle and overt tactics.
2. Be the child of God that promotes forgiveness and unity in the church, preventing the enemy from exploiting unresolved conflicts.
3. Equip yourself with the full armor of God (Ephesians 6:10–18) and stand firm against the devil's schemes.
4. Pray for discernment to recognize and counteract Satan's tactics.
5. Maintain a consistent prayer life, seeking God's guidance and strength.

We must watch out for the enemy's influence to cause us to disobey God. Adam and Eve's journey provides insight into the tactics of the serpent and the consequences of disobedience. The Bible says the serpent was the shrewdest of all the wild animals the Lord God had made. One day he asked the woman, "Did God really say you must not eat the fruit from any of the trees in the garden?"

"Of course we may eat fruit from the trees in the garden," the woman replied. "It's only the fruit from the tree in the middle of the garden that we are not allowed to eat."

God said, "You must not eat it or even touch it; if you do, you will die."

"You won't die!" the serpent replied to the woman. "God knows that your eyes will be opened as soon as you eat it, and you will be like God, knowing both good and evil." The woman was convinced. She saw that the tree was beautiful and its fruit looked delicious, and she wanted the wisdom it would give her. So she took some of the fruit and ate it. Then she gave some to her husband, who was with her, and he ate it too. At that moment, their eyes were opened, and they suddenly felt shame at their nakedness. So they sewed fig leaves together to cover themselves. Do you see the tactics of the enemy? He questions God's command: "Did God really say you must not eat the fruit from any of the trees in the garden?" sowing doubt in Eve's mind about what God said. The enemy distorts the truth, making it seem restrictive, causing Eve to reconsider. He contradicts the Word of God: "You won't die!" challenging God's authority and truthfulness. He appeals to desire, enticing Eve with the promise that eating the fruit will open her eyes and make her like God, knowing good and evil. "God knows that your eyes will be opened as soon as you eat it, and you will be like God, knowing both good and evil."

I have learned that anytime we submit to the enemy's tactics, there are consequences. Disobedience will cause us to experience a shake-up. The gift of God is eternal life, but the wages of sin are death! It may not be the termination of our time on earth; we may not die, but sin leads to something dying: a relationship, a work arrangement, a friendship, or your peace of mind.

Adam and Eve ate the forbidden fruit. Adam and Eve's decision to disobey introduced sin and death into the world. Their disobedience causes a separation from God. They became aware of their nakedness and felt shame, signifying a loss of innocence and purity. Expelled from the garden, they lost their direct access to God. Their choice to disobey God resulted in consequences for themselves and, unfortunately, for all of us. The ground is cursed, and Adam must toil for food. Eve is told she will experience pain during childbirth. But look at the love of God—how He intervenes and uses their act of disobedience to set the stage for His plan of redemption. The coming of Jesus Christ, who will ultimately defeat sin and death, restoring the relationship between God and us and qualifying us for heavenly citizenship, perhaps Jude said it best: "Now unto him that is able to keep you from falling and to present you faultless before the presence of his glory with exceeding joy, to the only wise God our Savior, be glory and majesty, dominion and power, both now and ever. Amen."

CHAPTER 3

# The Wheel of Deception

Remember, the "Wheel of Deception" is a metaphor for the cycles of confusion and misunderstanding that can ensnare us if we're not vigilant. It's a powerful image to illustrate how the enemy seeks to keep us trapped in patterns of thought, strongholds hindering our growth and preventing us from fully embracing the truth of God's kingdom. The illustration should help us understand that the enemy's strategies are not limited in their deployment. The cycles do not have to follow a strict progressive order; however, I firmly believe everything starts with diversion.

Diversion is a key strategy employed by the enemy to derail our spiritual journey. The enemy's goal is to pull our attention away from 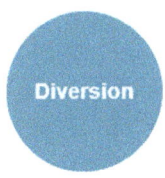 God's truth and His plans for our lives. By doing so, he weakens our relationship with God and impedes our growth. Understanding this strategy is crucial for maintaining a strong and focused faith. The enemy uses various methods to achieve his strategic intent.

Everyday concerns, entertainment, and worldly pursuits consume our time and energy, diverting our focus from God. Enticing us with sinful desires that lead us away from righteousness. Encouraging an emphasis on material success, personal ambition, and societal approval. The enemy's success is measured by the extent to which our relationship with God is negatively impacted.

If we allow distractions, temptations, and worldly pursuits to take precedence, our connection weakens, leading to less time spent in the presence of God. Should we fall into the pattern of failing to read and meditate on the Word, doubts and apathy set in. But, glory to God, despite the enemy's attempts to divert and deceive us, it is imperative to remember that he has already been defeated. Our loving God, showing us His mercy, provides hope and assurance in our spiritual battles.

The enemy was cast out of the presence of God; Jesus stripped him of any power he usurped from Adam. Colossians 2:15 affirms this: "And having spoiled principalities and powers, he made a shew of them openly, triumphing over them in it." As believers, we share in Christ's victory. Romans 8:37 declares, "Nay, in all these things we are more than conquerors through him that loved us."

The realization that we are more than conquerors, regardless of the enemy's strategies, is crucial for our resilience. We are empowered by the Holy Spirit to face any challenge with confidence.

An example of the enemy's modus operandi is seen in the story of Nehemiah, when he took on the task of rebuilding the walls of Jerusalem. He faced opposition from Sanballat, Tobiah, and Geshem, who were empowered by the enemy to cause diversion and hinder Nehemiah's mission. Nehemiah was greatly disturbed when he heard that Jerusalem was lying in ruins. When he arrived on the scene, he saw destruction everywhere. Empowered by the Spirit of God, he took on the enormous task of rebuilding, providing the leadership and determination required to complete the restoration in fifty-two days. Nehemiah turned to prayer and relied on his relationship with God for strength. Nehemiah 6:3, "I am doing a great work and I cannot come down." Our brother was focused and determined to stay on task despite the distractions. Similarly, in our own lives, prayer is our primary weapon to overcome any attempt by the enemy to cause a diversion. Paul emphasized this to the church at Corinth, reminding them and us that "the weapons of our warfare are not carnal but mighty through God to the pulling down of strongholds." Prayer helps us maintain our focus on God and His purposes. It connects us with God and releases Him to intervene. Through prayer, we resist the enemy's attempts to distract and divert us. We must recognize the importance of the work God has given us. Declare, "I am doing a great work and I cannot come down." Equip yourself with the full armor of God, remembering that our weapons are mighty through God to pull down strongholds. Embrace the truth that we are more than conquerors through Christ, facing any challenge with the confidence that the enemy has already been defeated.

The account of Jesus' temptation in the wilderness is an example of how the enemy uses temptation as a method to divert us from God's plan. After His baptism, Jesus was led by the Spirit into the wilderness to be tempted by the devil. He had fasted for forty days and nights and was hungry, making Him physically vulnerable. This period of testing highlights how the enemy attempts to exploit our weaknesses. It's important for us to understand the determination of the enemy. If one way doesn't work, don't be surprised by a return visit.

The enemy had three opportunities in his back pocket to divert Jesus from His destiny. The first pertained to physical needs. "If you are the Son of God, tell these stones to become loaves of bread." But Jesus told him, "No! The Scriptures say, People do not live by bread alone, but by every word that comes from the mouth of God." The enemy attempted to exploit Jesus' physical hunger to divert Him from reliance on God's provision. Jesus countered by affirming the supremacy of the Word of God as spiritual nourishment over physical needs. The second opportunity was pride and power. Then the devil took him to the holy city, Jerusalem, to the highest point of the Temple, and said, "If you are the Son of God, jump off! For the Scriptures say, 'He will order his angels to protect you. And they will hold you up with their hands, so you won't even hurt your foot on a stone.'"

Jesus responded, "The Scriptures also say, 'You must not test the Lord your God.'" This temptation sought to provoke Jesus into proving His divine identity through a dramatic display, appealing to pride and testing God's faithfulness. Jesus' response emphasized trust in God without demanding signs. In other words, Jesus knew who He was and didn't have to prove anything. Likewise, we are citizens of the kingdom of God and there's no expectation of us to prove it to the enemy upon his request. The third opportunity was the temptation of worldly authority and recognition. Next, the devil took him to the peak of a very high mountain and showed him all the kingdoms of the world and their glory. "I will give it all to you," he said, "if you will kneel down and worship me."

"Get out of here, Satan," Jesus told him. "For the Scriptures say, 'You must worship the Lord your God and serve only him.'" The offer of worldly power and recognition was not the enemy's to give; he didn't own anything; all things belong to Jesus. How stupid of the enemy to think Jesus didn't know His possessions were. It is so important for you and me to know who we are in the Lord Jesus Christ! Jesus reaffirmed His commitment to worship and serve God alone. Jesus' victory over temptation serves as a powerful example of how we, too, can remain steadfast and fulfill God's purposes for our lives.

In our spiritual journey, diversion is arguably the most insidious of the cycles we face. Once diversion takes hold, it becomes the root from which other detrimental cycles emerge. The enemy, subtle in his approach, infiltrates our daily routines, embedding his tactics within the mundane.

One of the most pervasive forms of diversion is social media. It's not unusual for a quick check of our phones to spiral into an hour of scrolling through Facebook, Instagram, or other platforms. This subtle consumption of time distracts us from more meaningful activities such as prayer, reading the Word, or spending time with the ones you love. I wonder: Do we have any idea of the cumulative time spent on social media daily? How often do we find ourselves engrossed in our phones within a given hour? If not social media, what about debt? Another area where diversion manifests. Debt can be a significant

# THE WHEEL OF DECEPTION

source of stress and anxiety for many, including those of us within the kingdom of God. Living with debt can lead to a relentless cycle of working overtime or a second job, thereby stealing precious time that could be spent in other ways. Are we living beyond our means, accumulating debt that could be avoided? God expects us to practice good stewardship of the resources He provides, even though we live in a society that equates happiness with material possessions. The pursuit of a newer car, a larger home, or a trendy wardrobe can quickly become a financial burden, leading us away from God. The more we chase after material things, the less we focus on exploring our rights as citizens of the kingdom of God. If these points resonate with you, it might be time to reevaluate priorities and seek contentment in God's provision. God encourages us to walk wisely, redeeming the time because the days are evil. This means being vigilant about how we spend our time and money.

Diversion can creep in unnoticed, but with intentionality, we can reclaim our focus and dedicate our lives more fully to God's purposes. Diversion is a subtle yet powerful tool the enemy uses to pull us away from God.

If you passed the social media and debt test, don't lose sight; the enemy can use other areas to create diversion, i.e., relationships, job, and other folks issues. Stay aware of his strategies and devices so he cannot spin us on the "Wheel of Deception." Let us commit to living intentionally, ensuring our focus remains steadfast on God's path. In all our ways, acknowledge God, and the Word says He will direct our paths.

Doubt can be a silent yet lethal adversary to our faith. If we open the door for seeds of doubt to be sown in our minds, causing us to question God's goodness and promises, this can lead to us questioning our identity, worth, and God's plan for our lives. The enemy tries to make us doubt God's inherent goodness by pointing to our struggles and hardships, enticing us to believe God is not truly good or that He does not care about our well-being. The enemy plants thoughts to make us question whether God's promises will actually come to pass. We may start to doubt the reliability of

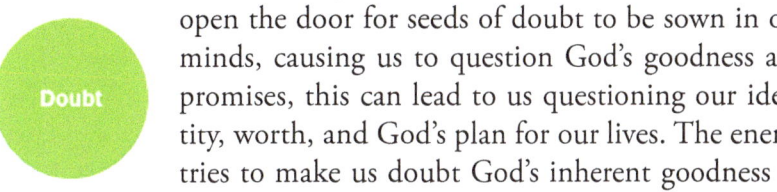

the Word and lose our faith grip. The enemy reminds us of past disappointments or unanswered prayers, eroding our trust in God and hindering our ability to rely on Him. Doubting God chips at the very foundation of our relationship with Him. Trust is essential in any relationship, and without it, our connection to God weakens. The Bible says, "It is impossible to please God without faith. Anyone who wants to come to him must believe that God exists and that he rewards those who sincerely seek him." Our relationship with God begins with the fundamental belief that He exists. This is the cornerstone of our faith. "For he that cometh to God must believe that He is." We must trust God! This trust reinforces our faith and provides the strength required to overcome doubt. Doubt is a powerful tool used by the enemy to undermine our relationship with God.

James's teaching on the dangers of doubt underscores the critical importance of unwavering faith. James 1:5–8 is worth our time to meditate. On this subject of doubting God, James lays out key points to help us avert this downfall. James begins by affirming God's generosity. When we need wisdom or anything else, we can confidently ask God, knowing He is willing to give generously and without rebuke. This encourages us to seek God openly and confidently in prayer, assured of His readiness to provide. Doubt signifies divided loyalty, making us as unstable as a wave of the sea, easily tossed by the wind. This instability reflects a lack of solid trust in God, leading to spiritual unreliability. James warns that those who doubt should not expect to receive anything from the Lord. Doubt hinders our prayers because it indicates a lack of complete trust in God's faithfulness and power. A person with divided loyalty is torn between trusting God and relying on worldly means or solutions. This division makes them unstable and unreliable in their faith journey and other aspects of life. Our prayer must be for the Holy Spirit to remind us frequently of God's faithfulness, generosity, and willingness to provide; daily regulate our heart and mind to identify areas of doubt; and should any doubt be recognized, we acknowledge it and bring it before God in prayer. Remember, faith is the cornerstone of our relationship with God. Doubt, instigated by the enemy, undermines this relationship and hinders us. Recognizing and resisting the enemy's lies ensures that our faith remains unwavering.

The story of Abraham and Sarah is a classic example of the dangers of doubting God and His promises. Their journey underscores the importance of waiting on God's timing and trusting His process. By learning from their experience, we can cultivate patience and trust in God's perfect timing, ensuring that we align our actions with His divine plan. God promised Abraham and Sarah a child, despite their advanced age and Sarah's lifelong inability to conceive. This divine promise filled them with a mix of incredulity and hope, challenging their faith and shaping the destiny of their descendants. God's promise seemed impossibly grand to Abraham and Sarah. When Sarah heard it, she laughed in disbelief, unable to imagine bearing a child at her advanced age. Abraham was seventy-five and Sarah was sixty-five when the promise was made. Over the next two decades, they waited. Each passing year tested their faith further, and the prolonged delay undoubtedly sowed seeds of doubt. They questioned if the promise would ever come to pass, grappling with their hopes and fears as they aged. Perhaps the extended wait for the promised child caused Abraham and Sarah to question:

- Maybe I didn't hear from God?
- Maybe I misinterpreted what God said?
- Maybe what I heard was the voice of my conscience?

Doubt led them to take matters into their own hands. Sarah suggested Abraham have a child with Hagar, her maidservant. Abraham did, and Ishmael was born. This decision, borne out of impatience and doubt, created immediate and long-term consequences. The immediate consequences were that Sarah's relationship with Hagar became strained, leading to tension and conflict in the house. Long-term consequences surfaced from ongoing conflict that impacted future generations, creating lasting strife between Ishmael's descendants and Isaac's lineage.

Despite their doubts and actions, God remained faithful. Sarah did give birth to Isaac when Abraham was one hundred years old and she was ninety. This miraculous fulfillment underscored God's faithfulness and perfect timing.

Here's my prayer for us: that we will secure the spiritual discernment the Lord has released to us and capture the lessons learned from this narrative. Abraham and Sarah teach us the importance of trusting God. I'm certain Abraham learned that moving ahead of God's plan leads to unnecessary complications and struggles. It's easy to become impatient and doubt God's timing, but we must remember to stay patient and faithful, trusting that God will fulfill His promises in His perfect timing.

Dear Lord, help us to mature in our relationship with You so that we may trust in Your perfect timing, even when it seems delayed. Teach us to understand that Your plans are always for our good and Your glory. Help us to resist the temptation to move ahead of You, and by doing so, we will avoid the complications that come with taking matters into our own hands. Strengthen our faith, so we may wait patiently on Your promises, knowing that You are faithful to fulfill them. Amen.

Doubt, like a shadow creeping across the mind, leads to an alarming sense of discouragement. Our belief in God wavers, leaving us to question the purpose and meaning behind life's trials. This uncertainty can be disheartening, creating a chasm between us and God. Yet, within this struggle lies the potential for growth. Through introspection and relying on the Spirit of God, we can discover that instead of discouragement eroding faith, it can fortify it. When we surrender to the Word of God, He transforms discouragement into a journey toward spiritual enlightenment. Sometimes, all that's needed is a shift in viewpoint—seeing the situation from a different perspective. I have learned that when confronted with discouragement, I have to relinquish, be still, and look to God for direction.

David faced a situation that seemingly left him discouraged. David and his men, coming home to Ziklag, found their city in ruins. The Amalekites swept through town, leaving nothing but ash and devastation in their wake. Ziklag, once a refuge, is now a smoldering skeleton of its former self. The sight of charred remains and the stench of burned wood filled the air. Even worse, their families—their wives, sons, and daughters—had been taken captive by the marauding Amalekites. The men were overcome with grief, their cries echoing through the desolate remains of their town. They wept until they had no strength left to weep. Among those taken were David's own wives, Ahinoam of Jezreel and Abigail, the widow of Nabal of Carmel. Despair hung heavily in the air, and the bitterness of the loss turned David's men against him. They talked among themselves about stoning David until he was dead. In his darkest moment, David turned to our God for strength and direction. He called for Abiathar, the priest, the son of Ahimelek. "Bring me the ephod," he instructed. With the sacred garment in place, David inquired of the LORD, "Shall I pursue this raiding party? Will I overtake them?"

The *Lord's* answer came clear and resolute: "Pursue them. You will certainly overtake them and succeed in the rescue."

This is a powerful example of shifting your viewpoint. Shift from the devastation to the wisdom of our God. Emboldened by God's assurance, David rallied his six hundred men and set off in pursuit of the Amalekites. They marched until they reached the Besor Valley, where exhaustion overcame two hundred of his men, leaving them unable to continue. David pressed on with the remaining four hundred. In a field, they stumbled upon an Egyptian, barely alive, abandoned by his Amalekite master. The men gave him water and food. Revived by their kindness, the Egyptian revealed his plight: "I am the slave of an Amalekite. My master left me behind when I fell ill three days ago. We raided territory belonging to Judah and Caleb. We burned Ziklag." David asked, "Can you lead me to this raiding party?"

"Swear to me before God that you will not kill me or hand me over to my master, and I will take you to them," the Egyptian pleaded. David agreed, and the Egyptian led them to the Amalekites, who were spread out across the countryside, celebrating their plunder with feasting and revelry. Seizing the moment, David and his men launched a surprise attack at dusk, fighting relentlessly until the evening of the next day. The battle was fierce, but ultimately decisive. Not a single Amalekite survived, except for four hundred young men who escaped on camels. In the aftermath, David surveyed the scene. Miraculously, everything the Amalekites had taken was recovered. His wives were safe, as were all the other captives. Not a single person was missing—young or old, boy or girl. Along with their loved ones, all the plunder was retrieved. David and his men, victorious and relieved, gathered their loved ones and possessions, carrying everything back to Ziklag. They had not only reclaimed what was theirs but also reaffirmed their faith and resilience in the face of adversity.

Discouragement, if allowed to fester, can lead us down a path we never intended to tread. It is a subtle thief, stealing our hope and paralyzing our spirit. At its core, discouragement is simply the absence of courage—the courage to rise after we fall, the courage to voice our truths, and to lift our eyes and trust in the God of our salvation. When we face setbacks, it is easy to succumb to despair and let the weight of our troubles anchor us in place. But this is precisely when courage must rise within us. Courage is not the absence of fear but the decision to act in spite of it. It is our inner strength that urges us to get up when we've been knocked down, to speak up when silence feels safer, and to look up to the heavens when our gaze is fixed on the ground. David lived by this truth. When David and his men returned to find their home destroyed and their loved ones taken captive, their initial reaction was one of utter despair. They wept until they had no strength left. Yet, in this moment of deepest sorrow, David chose to seek strength in the *Lord*, his God. He found the courage to inquire of God, to pursue the raiders, and ultimately to recover everything that had been lost. This story teaches us that discouragement need not be the end of our journey. Instead, it can be the catalyst for a renewed reliance on God, His strength, and His guidance. By looking up and trusting the God of our salvation, we find the courage to confront our challenges, to reclaim what was lost, and to continue moving forward with hope and determination. Discouragement is a temporary state of mind, but courage is a choice we can make every day. When we choose courage, we align ourselves with the infinite possibilities that faith in God provides. We become resilient, unstoppable, and victorious, no matter the obstacles we face.

There's one other point we must talk about, and that is that we have to do what is necessary to escape the long and detrimental reach of discouragement. You and I must take action, praying and seeking direction from God instead of waiting for someone else to do it for us. No, when no one else is around or seems to care, we need the resolve to seek God's face for ourselves and overcome the spirit of discouragement.

When we experience delays in life, it often brings feelings of frustration and impatience, which the enemy exploits to make us doubt God's promises. By understanding and aligning our timing with God's timing, we can overcome these challenges. Abraham and Sarah provide a powerful example of how even the most faithful can struggle with this alignment yet ultimately find strength in God's plan. God's timing, often referred to as divine timing, is the belief that everything happens at the right moment according to His plan. Unlike our own sense of timing, which is influenced by immediate desires and societal pressures, divine timing operates on a higher, more comprehensive understanding of our lives and the universe. This concept encourages trust and patience, knowing that God's plans are ultimately for our good, even if they don't align with our immediate expectations. During periods of delay, the enemy sows seeds of doubt, making us question whether God's promises will ever be fulfilled. This mindset can lead to actions outside of God's will.

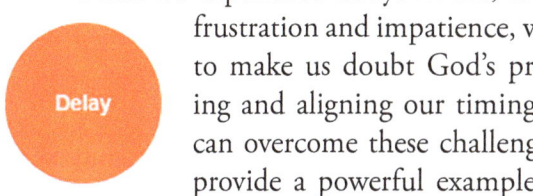

For example, we might start to believe that God has forgotten us or feel pressured to take matters into our own hands. Scripture provides numerous examples of this struggle. In our daily lives, we might experience it through thoughts of inadequacy or pressure from others to expedite processes requiring patience. Recognizing these tactics is the first step in combating them. Developing strategies like regular prayer, meditating on scripture, and surrounding ourselves with a supportive faith community can strengthen our faith and patience. Isaiah 40:31 offers a timeless message of hope and encouragement, emphasizing the extraordinary benefits of trusting in the Lord. The verse promises renewed strength to those who wait upon the Lord, using the powerful metaphor of eagles to illustrate how God empowers His followers to rise above their challenges. Just as eagles soar effortlessly through the sky, believers are assured they will run without growing weary and walk without fainting, a testament to God's sustaining power and endurance. This blessed assurance serves as a beacon of hope, reminding us of the boundless energy and support available to those who rely on Him. Imagine the majestic wings of an eagle, strong and unwavering, lifting you above life's trials. David endured approximately fifteen years between being anointed by Samuel as Israel's next king and finally ascending to the throne. During this period, he faced numerous trials, including fleeing from King Saul's relentless pursuit, living as a fugitive, and rallying a loyal but ragtag group of followers. Despite the uncertainty and danger, David's faith and resilience grew, preparing him for the monumental role that awaited him. This extended wait not only tested his patience but also shaped his character, making his eventual kingship all the more meaningful.

Noah waited 120 years while painstakingly building the ark, a massive undertaking that required immense faith and perseverance. Throughout this period, he faced ridicule and disbelief from those around him. Despite the scorn and isolation, Noah remained steadfast, trusting in God's warning of the impending flood. His unwavering dedication is a testament to his faith, underscoring the depth of his trust in God's promise.

Esther patiently and courageously waited for the right moment to approach the king, knowing that her request could mean life or death. In the face of the potential extermination of her people, she navigated the treacherous politics of the royal court with wisdom and resolve. Her bravery and patience not only saved her people from a tragic fate but also highlighted her strength and resilience.

Elizabeth and Zechariah, righteous in God's sight, faced the deep sorrow of childlessness despite their faithfulness. Their unwavering trust in God was rewarded in their old age with the miraculous birth of John the Baptist, a prophet who heralded the coming of the Messiah. Their journey from sorrow to joy serves as a powerful narrative of faith, patience, and divine intervention.

Jacob's love for Rachel and his perseverance amid deception illustrate the immeasurable impact of dedication and patience. After

## THE WHEEL OF DECEPTION

working fourteen years to marry Rachel, Jacob's commitment led to the formation of the twelve tribes of Israel, marking a significant milestone in the lineage of the Israelites.

What do these narratives have in common? Each highlights the challenge of waiting on God's timing amid trials. The enemy seeks to exploit these delays to sever our relationship with God. However, these stories validate that God exceeds our expectations in ways we can't even imagine. David's journey from anointment to kingship was a period of significant personal growth and preparation. The trials he faced and overcame were instrumental in shaping him into a leader chosen by God, ready to lead with wisdom, strength, and faith. Noah's steadfast faith and perseverance amid ridicule illustrate the depth of trust required to follow divine commands. His legacy is a reminder of the rewards of steadfast faith and perseverance in fulfilling God's promises. Esther's strategic patience and unyielding courage in saving her people serve as a timeless reminder of the power of bravery and resilience. Elizabeth and Zechariah's story of faith and divine intervention highlights the rewards of faithful waiting and the value of trusting God's perfect timing. Jacob's long years of labor and unwavering commitment demonstrate the power of love and perseverance in achieving one's destiny.

"But they that wait upon the *Lord* shall renew their strength; they shall mount up with wings as eagles; they shall run and not be weary; they shall walk and not faint. Why sayest thou, O Jacob, and speakest, O Israel, My way is hid from the *Lord*, and my judgment is passed over from my God? Hast thou not known? Hast thou not heard that the everlasting God, the *Lord*, the Creator of the ends of the earth, fainteth not, neither is weary? There is no searching of His understanding. He giveth power to the faint, and to them that have no might He increaseth strength." Amen.

The state of despair is an overwhelming feeling of hopelessness and loss. Triggered by various personal or external circumstances that seem insurmountable, despair can make us feel trapped and convinced that suffering will never end. This emotional state significantly impacts our mental, physical, and emotional well-being. Despair is not just a physical struggle; it is often a battle of the spirit. The enemy seeks to deceive us, leading us to digress and sink further away from the love and care of our God. In this state, we feel isolated and abandoned, losing sight of God's support and strength. Despair, much like severe depression, can derail our lives and rob us of the blessings and benefits of being citizens of God's kingdom. However, even in the deepest despair, there is hope. God's love and care are ever-present, offering solace and a path to recovery. Remember, you are not alone; God's support is always available, ready to lift you from the depths of despair. If you find yourself in a state of despair, consider reaching out to someone you trust, engaging in prayer, or reading scriptures that remind you of God's promises. Reflect on moments in your life where you felt God's presence and strength, and let these memories guide you back to hope. Despair may feel all-encompassing, but it is not the end. By recognizing God's unwavering love and seeking His comfort, you can find the strength to overcome and reclaim the blessings meant for you. Let this be a reminder that, even in your darkest moments, hope is always within reach.

The book of Ruth presents a compelling narrative of despair. Naomi experienced significant mental anguish after the deaths of her husband and two sons. Naomi's husband, Elimelech, dies, leaving her in a foreign land with their two sons. This initial loss sets the stage for the deepening of her grief. Her sons, Mahlon and Kilion, marry Moabite women, Orpah and Ruth, but both sons die ten years later. Naomi is left without immediate family support, a dire situation for a woman in ancient times. Being in Moab, Naomi faces the challenges of isolation and cultural dislocation, compounding her grief. In ancient society, a woman's security and identity were closely tied to her husband and sons. Naomi's losses stripped her of these protections, leaving her vulnerable. Naomi's decision to change her name to Mara, meaning "bitter," symbolizes her internal state of despair. This name change reflects her perception that God has dealt harshly with her. Naomi expressed a sense of being forsaken by God, viewing her misfortunes as a direct consequence of divine displeasure. Naomi decided to return to Bethlehem after hearing that the Lord had provided food for His people. This decision marks the beginning of her journey from bitterness to eventual restoration. Ruth's insistence on staying with Naomi: "Where you go, I will go, and where you stay, I will stay. Your people will be my people, and your God, my God" (Ruth 1:16), provides Naomi with companionship and support. Naomi made every attempt to influence Ruth not to stay; drowning in despair, Naomi failed to see Ruth as God's intervention. Ruth's loyalty and hard work played a crucial role in Naomi's path to emotional and social restoration. Boaz's kindness toward Ruth extended to Naomi, as he became a kinsman-redeemer, securing their future. The birth of Obed, Ruth's and Boaz's son, restored joy to Naomi. The women of Bethlehem acknowledge Naomi's restoration by saying, "Naomi has a son!" Obed's birth symbolizes the renewal of Naomi's life and the continuation of her family line, ultimately leading to the lineage of King David and Jesus.

Naomi is a powerful testament to the resilience of a woman of God in the face of intense loss and bitterness. Her journey from desolation to joy illustrates the themes of loyalty, divine providence, and redemption. Through the unwavering support of Ruth and the kindness of Boaz, Naomi's life is transformed, highlighting that even in the darkest times, hope and renewal are possible. "The state of despair is treacherous, but it does not hold supreme power. By trusting in God with all our heart and not relying solely on our own understanding, we empower God to guide our steps toward brighter days and lives fulfilled by His grace."

CHAPTER 4

# Wheel of Deception Out of Service

If you can relate to this writing, you are on the wheel, and each day it seems as though life is even more challenging. I got good news: the "Wheel of Deception" has an emergency stop, which, when pressed, renders it out of service. Through His sacrificial blood, our Lord and Savior Jesus Christ has the authority to disengage this "Wheel of Deception." Colossians 2:15 states, "And having spoiled principalities and powers, he made a shew of them openly, triumphing over them in it." The spoilage described here includes the "Wheel of Deception." Another way to think about it is to imagine a mechanism installed on a bicycle tire to prevent its movement. Envision that type of mechanism applied to the spokes of the "Wheel of Deception," preventing its cycles from operating.

In his first letter to the Corinthians, the Apostle Paul addresses the resurrection of Jesus Christ and its significance for us. He concludes with an encouragement: "But thanks be to God! He gives us the victory through our Lord Jesus Christ." This victory, won through Jesus Christ, is both a future promise and a present reality, empowering us to live victoriously. Paul urges us to remain steadfast and immovable: "Therefore, my dear brothers and sisters, stand firm. Let nothing move you." This calls for a deep-rooted stability in the truth of the gospel, a resilience against external pressures and internal doubts. Moreover, Paul encourages us to "always give ourselves fully to the work of the Lord." This is not a call for sporadic efforts but for continuous and enthusiastic engagement in God's work. Paul assures us that our commitment to the Lord in this way is not in vain and has eternal significance.

In a world full of distractions and challenges, maintaining steadfastness and immovability in faith is crucial. Recognizing and thanking God for the victory over sin and death through Jesus Christ transforms our outlook and provides a strong foundation for our faith journey. As citizens of the kingdom of God, embracing these truths enables us to live our faith with confidence, joy, and a sense of eternal purpose. Reflect on your own life. In what areas do you see the 'Wheel of Deception' at work? How can you apply the victory Christ has won to these areas? By doing so, we can triumphantly avoid the snares of the enemy and stay free of the vicious cycles of diversion, doubt, discouragement, delay, and despair.

Dear Lord, we need your help, your guidance, your grace, your mercy, and your peace. Father, we thank you for loving us as only you can; none has or will ever demonstrate a love for us that is comparable to your love. You provide for our needs, comfort us in our sorrows, and guide us through life's challenges. Now, Father, you have made us understand that we are in the world but not of the world. Lord, we recognize the Wheel of Deception is a reality for many, and the enemy desires us to become entangled in its vicious cycles. Thank you for the victory we have in Jesus, our Lord, and for the confidence we have in you to alert us when we are drifting and making ourselves vulnerable to the tactics of the enemy. Forgive us, Lord, for the times we have strayed and allowed ourselves to be deceived. Strengthen our resolve to stay focused on you and your truths. We are grateful for the constant reminders of your love and protection. Lord, we will forever love you, and today, we recommit our total being to you. By the grace you have imparted to us, we boldly declare that we are citizens of Your kingdom forevermore. Our profession stands on the authority of Jesus Christ, your son, our Lord! Amen!

Perhaps you have been reading this revelation, and you sense the nudging of the Holy Spirit saying to you that you need to engage in a relationship with the God of your salvation. Permit me to humbly submit: God has provided you with the way to engage with Him. It is through Jesus Christ. You may be wondering why there is so much emphasis on Jesus. You may have noticed some people act as though Jesus is a character in a story. No, He's more than that; He's the son of the Most High God. John 1 has us to understand that in the beginning was the Word, the Word was God, and the Word was with God; John then declares the Word became flesh; that's Jesus! I know this concept does not align with logic, but can I tell you that God is above logic? God has the power to defy logic. Think about it; Jesus's mother was a virgin; that's not logical. Jesus lived as a human, the same as us, and He never did anything wrong; He never had a thought about wrong; that's not logical. Our God defies logic; He is majestic; He is truth; He is grace; He is mercy; He is our creator and salvation. While He defies logic, He has a supernatural love for us and desires us to initiate a relationship with Him. Certainly, He has the power to make us love Him, but no, He wants us to voluntarily love and worship Him once we come to the knowledge of who He is and the degree of love He has for us. God is amazing; why not take Him up on this? I did, and I'll humbly tell you that when I did, God transformed my life. I want you to experience God as I have, and you can! How, you ask? Believe in Jesus and accept Him as God's Son, the Son that has delivered us from everything that is not of God and whose blood washes and cleanses us from everything that would prevent us from having this relationship with God. Perhaps now your question is: What do I do to start the relationship? Romans 10:9–10 tells us that if you will speak this out of your mouth, Lord Jesus, I believe that you are the Son of God; I believe God exists and has sent you; I accept you right now as my Lord and Savior; I understand my acceptance of You grants me access to kingdom citizenship; and from this day forward, I am saved and covered by your blood that was shed on the cross of Calvary for my sins. I love you, Lord, and willfully submit to you as the God of my life. Father God, in Jesus's name, I pray. Amen.

    Welcome to the family; enter into the presence of Almighty God with thanksgiving and adoration, recognizing that He is our Father, our Lord, and our God. Begin each day by acknowledging God's greatness and expressing gratitude for His blessings. Recognize that He is the foundation of our lives and the source of all good things. Enter the family with the expectation that God will honor His Word. Trust that God will fulfill His promises. His Word is exalted above His name, ensuring that what He has spoken will come to pass without fail. What He promises you and everyone else who accepts Jesus as their Lord and Savior, He will deliver. Every promise made in the Bible is a commitment from God that He will not break. His Word is a solid foundation upon which we can build our faith. Enter the family, approaching God with confidence, knowing that when we ask according to His will, He listens. By believing in His faithfulness and power, we can trust that our prayers will be answered. Embrace the gift of salvation through Jesus Christ with a heart full of faith. As members of God's family, we are assured of His unwavering support and love. Welcome to a journey of faith, where God's promises guide us, His love sustains us, and His faithfulness never fails.

# ABOUT THE AUTHOR

Pastor Madison C. Brown is married to Mrs. Zella Brown. Over the course of more than forty years, Pastor Brown and Zella have built a life filled with faith, love, and resilience. Together, they've raised four children who, in turn, have blessed them with five grandchildren. Their bond, rooted in shared devotion, continues to be a source of inspiration to their community.

Pastor Brown graduated from Faulkner University, Montgomery, Alabama, where his studies in theology and leadership laid the foundation for his lifelong ministry. Over the course of forty years, he has been privileged by God to serve as the senior pastor for five congregations:

- First Missionary Baptist, Decatur, Alabama
- First Missionary Baptist, Hartselle, Alabama
- Eleventh Street Baptist, Texarkana, Arkansas
- The Word Church, Texarkana, Texas
- St. Peter Missionary Baptist, Decatur, Alabama

In each congregation they served, Pastor and Mrs. Brown have faithfully relied on God's anointing to offer spiritual leadership, guidance, and support. Their ministry has touched countless lives—through heartfelt sermons, compassionate counseling, and community outreach efforts—all while teaching the enduring Word of God, which will never fade away.

Pastor Brown maintained a bivocational career, balancing his pastoral duties with a thirty-year role in Human Resources across the Paper and Pet Food industries. Managing HR departments in three paper mills in Alabama, Arkansas, and Georgia, Pastor Brown drew upon his leadership skills and empathy to foster positive workplace environments and mentor countless individuals. His final role at the J. M. Smucker Pet Food Plant in Decatur, Alabama, allowed him to retire with a deep sense of accomplishment, having successfully balanced his corporate career with his calling to ministry. His experiences in both realms strengthened his ability to connect with working families and support their spiritual and professional lives alike.

Pastor Brown maintains a deep passion for teaching God's Word while actively engaged in community and social justice initiatives. Brown has authored three books—*The Wheel of Deception, God's Liberating Power Demolishing Strongholds,* and *The Perils of Unbelief*—all of which are currently in the process of being published. In his free time, Pastor Brown enjoys reading and cherishing quiet moments with his beloved wife, Zella, as they support their children and grandchildren. Outside of family and faith, those who know him well are aware of his competitive streak on the pool table. He currently plays in the North Alabama Independent Pool League, where his teams have proudly earned the title of 2024 8-ball and 10-ball champions. This passion for pool, like his ministry, showcases his thoughtful, strategic approach to both life and leisure.